ISLE OF MAN
ROAD SERVICES

Richard Davis

Lily
Publications

Introduction

2016 is the 40th anniversary of the formation of Isle of Man National Transport when the Isle of Man's two bus fleets, Douglas Corporation Transport and Isle of Man Road Services, were amalgamated under government control.

Having dealt with Douglas Corporation buses in a previous volume, this work features the famous 'red buses' of Isle of Man Road Services.

Primarily operating outside Douglas, the Road Services' fleet was once a familiar sight on Manx roads and covered a comprehensive network of routes which reached all but the most remote corners of the Island.

Always maintained in a smart and tidy condition, Road Services gave sterling service to the Isle of Man from the late 1920s until nationalisation in October 1976.

Viewed with great affection by both residents and visitors to the Island, the operation was also highly regarded by other transport undertakings throughout the UK and beyond, many of which were considerably larger organisations operating huge fleets.

It has been an honour and a pleasure to have known many of the Road Services' staff over the years and to have the opportunity to drive some of the buses, and indeed to own one, a 1967 Leyland Leopard, which appears later in the book.

My sincere thanks to all who have helped with information and photographs, most particularly Mike Lambden whose late father Bill Lambden was the General Manager of Isle of Man Road Services from 1965 to 1976. Thanks also to my eagle-eyed proof-reader Samantha Thorpe and, as always, Miles Cowsill of Lily Publications.

Richard Davis

PHOTOGRAPHS: *Images for the book were sourced from the author's collection (AC), Stan Basnett (SB), the late Bill Lambden's collection (ML), John Davis (JD), Ray Stanfield (RS), Manx National Heritage (MNH) and Travel Lens Photographic (TLP)*

In this 1960 view, Leyland Titan PD3/3 No. 33, which was new in 1958, poses in Peveril Square, Douglas with the Victoria Pier Arcade as a backdrop. Demolition of the arcade started the following year and the Sea Terminal which replaced it opened in 1965. (MNH)

Published by Lily Publications IOM Ltd
Copyright © 2016. All rights reserved.
ISBN 978-1-911177-08-1

A pair of immaculate Thornycroft BCs pose in the forecourt of
Douglas Railway Station. Nearest the camera is MN 5454, new in
1928 to Isle of Man Railway and originally operated in their blue
livery as fleet number 13. (SB)

Castletown Railway Station is the location for this view of ADC 416A MN 4929 which had been new to Manxland Bus Services in 1927. The bus was taken over by Isle of Man Railway in 1929, receiving fleet number 25. (SB)

The Isle of Man's first motor 'buses' were a pair of Argus charabancs which started a service in 1907 with the Manx Electric Railway between the Bungalow on the Snaefell Mountain Railway and the company's hotel and tea-rooms at Tholt-y-Will.

This was followed by Douglas Corporation Tramways' first motor buses in 1914 (see Douglas Corporation Buses in Pictures – Centenary Edition).

No other stage services ran elsewhere on the Island until 1927 when Manxland Bus Services commenced operation, quickly followed by three other companies - Farghers Omnibuses, Manx Motors and P. Richmond Ltd.

The Isle of Man Railway Company evidently saw the buses as a threat to their near-monopoly of public transport and took over Farghers in 1928, operating under the fleet name "Isle of Man Road Services". Allan Mylchreest Sheard, who had worked for the railway company since 1909 and who had been involved in motor transport in the army during the First World War, was appointed Secretary and Manager (later General Manager).   The following year, the Railway bought out Manx Motors and Manxland while P. Richmond Ltd. ceased trading, leaving Isle of Man Railway in possession of most of the bus route network outside Douglas.

 Photo: A.M. Sheard - Isle of Man Road Services' first Secretary and Manager. (Photographer unknown).

A more formal arrangement followed in 1930 when Isle of Man Road Services Ltd was formed as a company - a subsidiary of Isle of Man Railway.

Having inherited a varied collection of 81 vehicles, Road Services set about establishing a more unified fleet that was to form the basis of operations for years to come. For the most part, the amalgamated fleet adopted the former Manxland red and cream livery in place of Manx Motors broken white and Isle of Man Railway blue though several of the latter escaped repainting and continued to wear blue livery throughout their service lives.

Manx Motors' fleet of new buses lined up at Peveril Square, Douglas in 1927. (AC)

Right: One of Manxland's Guy BBs, MN 5042, No. 18, in Lord Street, Douglas circa 1927. (RS)

An early view inside Homefield Garage, built by Manxland, in Salisbury Street, Douglas. Thornycroft BC MN 5456 No.16, new to Isle of Man Railway in 1928 is in the centre. Another Thornycroft, No.13, is behind, while to the right is AEC 202, MN 5108, still in Manxland livery but carrying IMR fleet number 51. On the far left is an ADC 416A MN 5505, new to Manx Motors in 1928 and wearing Road Services' fleet number 75. (SB)

A 1929 scene at Douglas Railway Station showing Leyland PLSC3 Lion MN 5584, (right) new to Manxland in 1928 and still wearing Manxland livery and fleet name but carrying Isle of Man Road Services' fleet number 42. On the left is Thornycroft BC MN 5942 new to Isle of Man Railway in 1928, carrying Isle of Man Road Services' fleet number 53. (SB).

Two views of former Manx Motors Thornycroft A2 MN 5005 operating as Road Services' No. 60. New in 1927, it was one of those acquired by Isle of Man Railway in 1929, receiving a repaint into IMR blue livery which it carried for the rest of its service life. In these photos, it still looks tidy shortly before withdrawal from service in 1951. (ML)

Above: While several old buses lived on for a time as hen houses or circus caravans, this Leyland Lion PLSC1 which had been new to Manxland Bus Services in 1927 ended up derelict at St Johns after withdrawal in 1950 and was finally scrapped in 1958. (AC)).

Right: Probably dating from circa 1948/9, this photo shows ADC 416As parked at the rear of Ramsey Bus Station when all four were withdrawn and awaiting scrapping. From left to right: No. 76 MN 5506, No. 77 MN 5507, No. 80 MN 5510 and No. 30 MN 4928. All were new in 1927/8 to Manxland Bus Services. (ML)

Isle of Man Railways acquired a considerable number of Thornycroft A2s from Manx Motors and also obtained some new ones in their own right in 1928.

Above: A2, No. 20, MN 5461, pictured at Port Erin, was withdrawn from service in 1953 and is one of the buses that became a circus caravan. (AC)

Right: Rear views are something of a rarity, making this photo of another A2, No. 22, MN 5453 all the more interesting. (AC)

Left: Ex-Manxland Leyland Lion PLSC3 MN 5584, which dated from 1928, was acquired by the railway company in 1929. It became Road Services' No. 42 and continued in service until 1951. In this view, it is seen parked alongside Ramsey Bus Station which had been built by Manxland in 1927. (ML)

Below: Road Services operated no less than 21 Thornycroft BCs, two of which, MN 5456, No. 16 and MN 5462, No.1 are pictured in this Ramsey view. (RS)

A view inside Homefield Garage showing Leyland Lion PLSC3 No. 32, MN 5943. New to Manxland Bus Services in 1928, it was taken over by Isle of Man Railway in 1929 and subsequently continued with Road Services until it was withdrawn in 1951. To the right is PD1 No. 8, GMN 778 which dates from 1947 and was the only one of its type to have a chromed radiator surround – the remainder of the batch all being painted. (AC)

Above: Thornycroft BC MN 5464, No. 3, pictured in Lord Street, Douglas at the junction with Ridgeway Street. New to the railway company in 1928, it operated with the Road Services' fleet name with the illuminated three legs symbol above the destination box. (RS)

Left: Port Erin is the location for this view of two Thornycroft BCs towards the end of their lives. Both were new to Isle of Man Railway. On the left is MN 5943 No. 54, new in 1929, while to the right is MN 5942, No. 53 which had been a demonstrator prior to acquisition by the company in 1928. They lasted in passenger service until 1953 and 1950 respectively and both were subsequently used as Road Services' towing vehicles. (AC)

In 1934, Road Services began ordering new buses as opposed to those it had inherited from its predecessors. The first to arrive were five modern-looking Leyland Lion LT5As fitted with Northern Counties 28-seat bodywork. These were MN 5071, 5107, 9498 and 9499 - numbered 56, 50, 35, 67 and 74. From this time onward and indeed right to the end of the company's existence, Leyland vehicles were to be predominant in the fleet.

Right: MN 9498, No. 35 is pictured in Lord Street which was the Douglas terminus prior to moving to the site adjacent to the Clarendon Hotel following major clearances of old buildings between North Quay and Duke Lane in the early 1930s. (RS)

In the second view, 35 pauses in Main Road, Kirk Michael en-route from Ramsey to Douglas via Peel. (ML)

Fast-forward a few years to this scene inside Homefield Garage showing Leyland Lion LT5A No. 50, MN 5107; Lion PLSC1 No. 117 MN 5105, (originally No. 27 in the Manxland fleet), and PD2/1 No. 63, KMN 513. Lion No. 50, which was new in 1934, had been withdrawn from service in 1955 but was stored until 1967 when it was sold to a farm at Ronague. Lion No. 117 had been withdrawn in 1951 and subsequently saw another sixteen years' service as a tree-lopper. (AC)

Though Leyland became the preferred marque, there were occasional interlopers such as this AEC Regal 4 with Burlingham bodywork pictured outside Ramsey Bus Station. An AEC demonstrator bought by Road Services in 1934, No. 51 was one of several buses to be stored following withdrawal pending a decision as to their future. Withdrawn from service in 1955, it was eventually passed to a scrap dealer in 1961 and ended up as a hen-house. (ML)

The next new deliveries, in 1935, were three Leyland Lion LT7s, MAN 450-452, (fleet numbers 59, 61, 69), this time with Leyland bodywork, followed by a Commer PN3 in 1936.

The Commer, which received fleet number 41, had Waveney 14 seat bodywork and was painted in special 'airline' livery of silver and blue to operate a dedicated Douglas to Ronaldsway Airport service. (ML)

Also acquired in 1936 as a consequence of Road Services taking over the business of W.N. Cowin of Andreas, was a Thornycroft A6, MN 7858, which was issued fleet number 34. It was used for a time on services to Hall Caine Airport at Close Lake in the north of the Island but following the cessation of scheduled services in 1937, the Thornycroft saw little use and it was withdrawn in 1940 and subsequently scrapped. Another new arrival, in 1937, was a Fordson V8 fitted with a Waveney 16 seat body, again intended for airport use. The Fordson received fleet number 44 and was registered CMN 75. It remained in service until 1953 when it was withdrawn and found further use as a circus caravan for a short time before being scrapped.

Leyland products once again came to prominence with the 1938 intake of six Leyland Lion LT9s, all with Leyland 28 seat bodywork. These were: 36-38, CMN 690-603 and 45-47, CMN 693-695.

Right: One of the 1938 Lion LT9s, No. 47, CMN 695, photographed in Main Road, Kirk Michael on its way to Douglas. (ML)

Below: Lion LT9s No. 47 and No. 37 at the rear of Ramsey Bus Station in 1963 at the end of their service lives. No. 37 had been withdrawn from service in 1962 and No. 47 was about to follow. Both look far too good to be used as hen-houses which is what became of them. (ML)

With the intervention of the Second World War in 1939, bus manufacturers turned to the production of military vehicles and aircraft so no new buses were to appear on Manx roads for several years. Older vehicles which would normally have been pensioned-off were kept going, but by 1945, vehicle reliability and condition was causing concern and a limited number of 'wartime-austerity' buses were made available to operators. In the case of Isle of Man Road Services, these took the form of six Bedford OWBs – GMN 145-150, taking fleet numbers 26-29 and 39-40. They carried rather plain Duple utility bodywork with 32 wooden seats and had the distinction of being the first one-man operated buses in the fleet.

Left and below left: Bedford OWB No. 29 shows off its angular lines while turning at Maughold Church. (ML)

Right: Interior view of OWB No. 29 – by the time this photograph was taken, the original wooden seats had been replaced with something a bit more comfortable. (ML)

Continuing the tradition of painting some of the fleet in airline livery, this view of Lord Street Bus Station shows Bedford No. 39 in British European Airways colours – Bedford No. 40 was similarly treated. All six of the Bedfords remained in service until 1966/67. (ML)

With the exception of a solitary Tilling-Stephens open-top double decker operated by Douglas Corporation Tramways from 1922, there were no double-deck buses in operation on the Island until 1933 when the Corporation began buying AEC Regent I double-deckers, acquiring a total of ten before the outbreak of World War II in 1939.

Meanwhile, regulations prevented Isle of Man Road Services from operating buses with more than 34 seats outside Douglas, though it did not prohibit the use of double-deckers. 1946 was the year that this changed when Road Services bought a Leyland Titan PD1 double decker, GMN 714, fitted with 56-seat Leyland bodywork. The bus was operated on the Onchan Circular route with all but the eight rearmost seats on the top deck boarded off, thus demonstrating how out-of-step the regulations were. The authorities quickly got the point and regulations were amended to permit the use of all seats.

Two images of Isle of Man Road Services' first double decker Leyland Titan PD1 No. 3, GMN 714 loaded and ready for shipping to the Isle of Man in August 1946. (AC)

Leyland Titan PD1 No. 11, GMN 780 of the same type introduced to the Island's roads by Road Services in 1946.

In these two 1947 photographs, the bus is loaded aboard the Steam Packet vessel *King Orry*, which itself had only entered service the previous year, ready for shipment to Douglas. (AC)

PD1 No.11 was eventually withdrawn from passenger service in 1972 and went on to become a mobile railway exhibition vehicle for the Kirk Michael Steam Centre. (AC)

Leyland Titan PD1 No. 11, GMN 780, still looks in remarkably good condition after around twenty years' service in this shot circa 1966. Of interest in the background is the Walpole Hotel, the Royalty Cinema (where Josef Karma the hypnotist is appearing) and the Sea Terminal with several porters' handcarts lined up in front. In the mid-distance, a Steam Packet Scammell mechanical horse is towing a ship's gangway with a member of staff aboard along Bath Place to the Steam Packet workshop in Fort Street. Note that despite the fairly heavy steering, the bus driver is steering with one hand while his right arm is extended through the cab window signalling a right turn. (AC)

In the next two years, Road Services bought more PD1s, raising the total to twelve. One of the PD1s, GMN 781, unfortunately had to be withdrawn prematurely following an incident at the junction of Circular Road and Peel Road in Douglas in August 1958 when the bus overturned. Of the remainder, most gave twenty years' service and a couple of them kept going until 1972. One of the PD1s saw further use as a tree-lopper and continued in use until 1977 in the Isle of Man National Transport fleet.

Left: PD1 HMN 726 was withdrawn from passenger service in November 1967 and converted for use as a tree-lopper. Originally carrying fleet number 23, it had been re-numbered 122 by the time this photo was taken in December 1967, showing the transformed vehicle emerging from Homefield Garage onto Salisbury Street. (MNH)

Following World War II, the single-deck fleet was also in urgent need of replacements. In this case, while chassis were available, such was the demand throughout the industry that no bodybuilder could be found to fit bodies. Not wishing to miss their chance of obtaining new chassis, Road Services bought four Leyland Tiger PS1s in 1946 and shipped them to the Island to be put into storage. Around eighteen months later, arrangements had been made for Eastern Coachworks of Lowestoft to assemble the bodywork and they were duly sent back across the Irish Sea for completion before returning once again to the Island.

Below: Pictured alongside Ramsey Bus Station, Leyland Tiger PS1s No. 58 and No. 34 show off their Eastern Coachworks bodywork to good advantage. (AC)

A 1955 view of Tiger No. 57, HMN 789 showing the sliding door fitted on the Eastern Coachworks body. All four Tigers were withdrawn in 1967. (ML)

Three of the Tigers became builders' site huts and were eventually scrapped while the fourth, No. 34, became an office at Port Erin Railway Station. Fortunately, it survived long enough to be secured for preservation. Above: Tiger No. 34, following withdrawal from passenger service, in use at an office at Port Erin. (AC)

Road Services' next addition to the fleet, in 1948, was a Bedford OB with bodywork by Mulliner. Very similar to the wartime Bedford OWBs but with more stylish coachwork, the OB took fleet number 25. It remained in service until 1965.

Lord Street Bus Station in 1953 – Left to right: Bedford OB No. 25, JMN 936, Leyland Lion LT9 No. 46, CMN 694 and Douglas Corporation Transport Leyland Cub No. 10, BMN 256. An unidentified Corporation Daimler CWA6 is on the far right while the Clarendon Hotel can be seen in the left background. (TLP)

Isle of Man Road Services embarked on a major fleet-renewal programme in February 1949 when they took delivery of eighteen Leyland Titan PD2s, KMN 500-517.

Right: In an unusual move, fifteen of the PD2s were shipped to the Island in one batch aboard a converted tank landing craft 'Empire Gaelic' with the other three arriving within days. (MNH).

Below: Leyland Titan PD2/1 KMN 503, adorned with Road Services livery and carrying fleet number 1, poses for a pre-delivery photograph during a test-run from the Leyland factory. (ML)

A view of PD2/1 No. 2 turning sharp left from Douglas Road onto Peel Road, Kirk Michael. The fleet name in block-shaded lettering is positioned on the 'tween-decks' panel. This was later re-designed and moved to the main side panel below the waist-rail. Note the offside front mudguard projecting well below the dash panel making the PD2s easily distinguishable from the PD1s – see earlier pictures. Though outwardly similar to the PD1s, they had a more powerful 9.8 litre engine as opposed to the 7.4 litre unit of the PD1s. (ML)

Leyland Titan PD2/1 No. 79 heads a line of similar buses at Lord Street Bus Station, Douglas. The fleet numbers originally issued to the batch of eighteen PD2s were as follows: KMN 500-502 (70-72), KMN 503-504) (1-2), KMN 505-512 (75-82), KMN 513-515 (63-65), KMN 516 (5), KMN 517 (9). (AC)

PD2/1 No. 82 with another member of the class waits for its next turn of duty at Lord Street Bus Station. This photo shows the revised fleet name on the side panels. In the background, one of Douglas Corporation Transport's AEC Regent IIIRTs can be seen on the Douglas Head route 25. (AC)

A rear view of PD2/1 No. 79 showing the company crest. The photo also shows the single rear light and absence of indicators fitted to the Leyland bodywork on these vehicles.
Many Road Services buses were supplied with the bare legal minimum of lighting (and no heaters!) and while some eventually acquired improved equipment, this did not always extend to the fitting of flashing indicators. (ML)

Leyland Titan PD2/1 No. 78 poses outside Laxey Bus Garage. The structure was originally built to house only single deck vehicles but following the acquisition of double-deckers in the 1940s, the roof was raised by several feet to accommodate them. (AC)

Among further new arrivals in 1950 were two more Bedford OBs with Mulliner bodywork. Registered LMN 147 and LMN 546, they were issued with fleet numbers 30 and 43.

Left: No. 30 inside Ramsey Bus Garage (AC)

Below: a 1964 view outside the Isle of Man Bank in Main Road, Kirk Michael. (ML)

No. 30 remained in service until 1967 following which it briefly became Isle of Man Railway parcels van No. 130 before being sold to Crowe Bros, builders of Kirk Michael. It was scrapped in 1972.

No. 43 was also taken out of service in 1967 and used as Isle of Man Railway parcels van No. 121. Final withdrawal from service came in February 1969 after which it became a hen-house at Abbeylands.

Bedford OB No. 43 looks very smart in this view taken at Lord Street Bus Station, Douglas. (AC)

Further deliveries of Leyland Titan PD2s occurred in 1950 with the arrival of MMN 11 and MMN 12 which received fleet numbers 13 and 14.
Above: One of the 1950 intake of PD2s, No.13, waits for its next duty at Lord Street Bus Station. Behind is PD1 No.11, GMN 778. (AC)

A 1967 view inside Homefield Garage in Salisbury Street, Douglas. PD2/1 No. 14, MMN 12, is flanked by another PD2, No. 72 on the right and on the left by one of the newly-arrived former Aldershot & District Dennis Falcons, POR 423, still in its previous owner's green livery. Opposite is Leyland Tiger PS1 No. 34 HMN 727 which had just been withdrawn from passenger service. (ML)

One of the first four Leyland/MCW Olympic HR40s, No. 48, MMN 298 in a pre-delivery photograph. Note the absence of a nearside mirror which remained to be fitted. (ML)

Radically different from anything previously seen on the Island's roads, the next purchases by Road Services, also in 1950, were four Leyland/MCW
Olympic HR40s registered MMN 296–299 with fleet numbers 17, 18, 48, and 49. The first part of an order for a total of eight buses, the Olympic model was named to mark the Olympic Games of 1948 held in London. They were the first 'integral' buses to come to the Isle of Man and also the first under-floor engined buses on the Island.

Chassis and body were usually chosen to suit the particular needs of the operator and while the PD2s, for example, had both chassis and body manufactured by Leyland Motors, this was by no means always the case. The Olympic, however, did not have this option and operators had to either take the Leyland/MCW combination or do without. Many chose to look elsewhere for vehicles and the Olympic consequently was a poor seller. In fact, Isle of Man Road Services was the best customer for the HR40 model (Home Range 40 seats).

Continuing to follow No. 48's career, it is next seen at Lord Street Bus Station, Douglas. Note that the fleet name had been re-styled and positioned on the side panel rather than the waist-rail. Although not readily apparent in this view, a nearside mirror has also been fitted. The bus is photographed against the backdrop of the Air Terminal/Bus Station building, opened in October 1962. One feature of these buses that did not endear them to drivers was an awkwardly placed handbrake, mounted to the left of the gear lever resulting in drivers having to step over it to get in and out of the cab. (AC)

Above: A further livery development shows No.48, again at Lord Street Bus Station, with the later style fleet name and larger fleet numbers. (AC)

Right: The sole survivor of the eight Road Services Leyland Olympics, No. 84 in later years at a UK vintage vehicle event. (JD)

Though not popular with UK bus operators, the Olympic was well-suited to the Isle of Man. Weighing a little over six and a half tons but with the same Leyland 9.8 litre engine as the PD2s, they had a very good power-to-weight ratio while averaging a fuel consumption of around 10.5 miles per gallon. The modest dimensions of the bodywork - 7' 6" wide x 27' 6" long – gave them a high degree of manoeuvrability on narrow country roads.

On the down-side, the vacuum brakes had to be carefully adjusted to obtain efficient braking and one former Road Services engineer recalls taking an Olympic for a test run from Homefield Garage and while descending Ballaquayle Road had intended to make a right turn into York Road. However, he had misjudged the braking capabilities of the bus and was obliged to take the next right turn into Waverley Road instead. Fortunately there was no other traffic around at the time…

In 1950, Road Services bought out Broadbent's of Ramsey Safeway bus service – the last independent bus operator on the Island. With the business, they acquired three former Safeway vehicles: FMN 934, a Bedford OWB, new in 1945; JMN 455, a 1947 Commer Commando with Waveney bodywork and KMN 938, a Bedford OL with Armoury bodywork which had been new the previous year.

These three took fleet numbers 86, 87 and 92 in the Road Services fleet, quickly losing their green and cream Safeway livery in favour of Road Services red and cream. The ex-Safeway trio remained as part of the Road Services fleet until 1965/66 when they were withdrawn.

Right: Ex Safeway Commer Commando No. 87, JMN 455 outside Peel Bus Station in 1964. (ML)

Centre: Ex Safeway Bedford OL No. 92, KMN 938 photographed in 1953. (TLP)

Below: Ex-Safeway Commer Commando No. 87 JMN455 pictured outside Homefield Garage in Salisbury Street, Douglas. (AC)

The second part of the Leyland/MCW Olympic order arrived in 1951 when MMN 300–303 joined the fleet, taking numbers 53 and 83-85. The eight Olympics were withdrawn between 1972 and 1975.

One of the second batch of Leyland Olympics, MMN 302, originally No. 84 and re-numbered 52 in October 1968, at Peveril Square, Douglas. (AC)

Two further PD2/1s joined the fleet in 1951 - NMN 361 and NMN 362. These took fleet numbers 62 and 66 though they were re-numbered 61 and 68 in July 1968.

PD2/1 No. 62 NMN 361 at Lord Street Bus Station. One of the Road Services buses transferred to Isle of Man National Transport in 1976 but not operated, No. 62 was converted to open top for use as a tree-lopper and remained in service until 1981. (AC)

NMN 361 and 362 were to be the last conventional exposed-radiator PD2s purchased, though some of the second-hand PD3s which followed had a similar frontal appearance as will be seen in later pages. (AC)

Main picture: PD2/1 No. 62, NMN 362 at Ronaldsway Airport. Remaining in service until 1976, the bus was withdrawn due to fire damage sustained while parked outside Homefield Garage.

Inset: Lower deck fire damage on PD2/1 No. 62 NMN 362 on 15 February 1976 which resulted in its withdrawal from service. The bus saw out its remaining years as a hay store at Church Farm, Malew. (AC)

A line-up of PD2/1s at the rear of Ramsey Bus Station in July 1974. From the left: No.74 is withdrawn awaiting disposal, No. 12 is still in service, No. 87 is withdrawn awaiting sale and No. 61 is still in service. The two still in service continued until October 1976 when they passed to Isle of Man National Transport but neither was operated by the new owner. (AC)

1952 saw the introduction of Road Services' first eight foot wide buses - four Leyland Royal Tigers fitted with 30 foot long Leyland 44-seat bodywork (later reduced to 40 seats), issued with fleet numbers 88-91 and registered NMN 906-909.

These had much the same running gear as the Olympics that preceded them but with separate chassis they could be fitted with bodywork of the operator's choice. The Royal Tigers were quite substantial vehicles and at seven and a half tons were almost a ton heavier than the Olympics – something that manifested itself in heavier steering. All four survived to be taken over by IOM National Transport in 1976 but they only lasted a year or two with the new undertaking before being withdrawn from service.

Leyland Royal Tiger No. 90, NMN 908 photographed in the UK prior to delivery. Note the revised fleet names introduced with these vehicles and subsequently applied to other members of the fleet. The polished aluminium trim fitted to these buses was removed during overhaul in later years resulting in a much less attractive appearance. (ML)

Royal Tiger No. 88 being transported to the Isle of Man in the usual way, across the bow of a Steam Packet ship. Note the detachable section of railing in front of the bus. When the tide was at the correct height – something which only lasted for a few minutes – the bus would be driven off onto the quayside over a pair of hefty 'planks' of wood. (ML)

Continuing to follow No. 88's progress, the Royal Tiger shows off its Leyland bodywork to good effect in this image taken at Lord Street, Douglas. In the background are Douglas Corporation AEC Regent III No.57 and Regent V No.75 with St Barnabas Church (demolished July 1969). (AC)

Royal Tiger No. 88 passed to Isle of Man National Transport in October 1976 and continued operating until withdrawal from passenger service in March 1978. It was subsequently used as staff transport for Isle of Man Railways as seen in this 1979 view at Douglas Railway Station. The absence of the polished aluminium body trim is very apparent, as is the replacement of the opening driver's windscreen with a one-piece windscreen glass. (AC)

There was a gap of four years before the next new arrivals, in 1956. These were three PD2/22s, TMN 334 – TMN 336 with fleet numbers 93-95. Visually very different from previous orders in that, at 27 feet, they were one foot longer and had enclosed-radiator bodywork of a lightweight design by Metropolitan Cammell Carriage and Wagon Co. - often referred to as 'tin-front' on account of the front panels being all-metal. Also noteworthy is the fact that for the first time, double deckers were delivered with a single cream band on the 'tween-decks' panel rather than three bands as hitherto applied, and A.M. Sheard's title in the legal lettering had changed to 'General Manager'.

Leyland Titan PD2/22 No.95 in a pre-delivery view. The differences between this design and earlier exposed-radiator PD2s can clearly be seen. Polished aluminium rear hubcaps were introduced with these buses and a link with tradition was maintained in that black mudguards were still featured. Like their predecessors, these PD2s had the Leyland 9.8 litre diesel engine but at almost a ton less unladen weight, their performance was noticeably livelier and fuel consumption figures were much improved. (ML)

Leyland Titan PD2/22 No.93 at Lord Street Bus Station. Of the three members of this batch, No.95 was withdrawn from service in 1974 while Nos. 93 and 94 were withdrawn in 1975 and ended their days at Jurby Garage. (AC)

PD2/22 No.94 leaves Peveril Square, Douglas for a trip round Onchan. In the right background, the Sea Terminal building (opened 1965) can be seen in the early stages of construction. (AC)

1957 saw the arrival of four more lightweight vehicles – Leyland Tiger Cubs WMN 5-8 with fleet numbers 19-22 and fitted with Weymann bodywork. These had the comparatively small Leyland O.350 5.76 litre engine and made up for the lack of power by having a two-speed rear axle, effectively giving eight forward gears and two reverse.

Although good fuel consumption figures were achieved - usually around 13 miles per gallon - they were not as good as might have been hoped, possibly due to the fact that the buses had to be driven hard to make satisfactory progress as they had little power in reserve.

A noteworthy feature of the Tiger Cubs is that they were the first vehicles in the fleet to be equipped with air brakes.

Tiger Cub No.20 looking very smart outside the Isle of Man Bank in Peel. Withdrawn from service in 1981, Tiger Cub No. 20 is the only survivor of the four members of the 1957 intake. (AC)

Tiger Cub No.21 shows the change of livery to grey and red livery received by 20-22 in 1969 (No. 19 remained red and cream) as part of Road Services' venture into coaching operations. Note the coach-type seats with which these buses were equipped as part of the conversion process. All three reverted to standard red and cream fleet colours in 1973 and bus seats were reinstated. (AC)

Leyland Tiger Cubs Nos. 8 and 5 (originally Nos. 19 and 22) in Peel Depot. Note the amended application of the cream band compared with the original livery and the replacement of the hinged driver's windscreen with one-piece fixed glass. Though Road Services' vehicles were normally maintained in good condition, Tiger Cub No.8 is obviously in need of some attention to the lower front bodywork. (AC)

New arrivals in 1958 were once again Leyland double-deckers and while of similar appearance to the PD2/22 'tin-fronts' Nos. 93-95, the new vehicles were PD3/3s.
These were fitted with 30 foot long bodywork by Metropolitan Cammell Carriage and Wagon Co and registered XMN 345-7 with fleet numbers 31-33.
In this and the following image, Leyland Titan PD3 No.31 is seen loaded aboard the Isle of Man Steam Packet vessel Snaefell at Fleetwood ready for shipment to the Isle of Man. (ML)

Above: Leyland PD3 No.33 at the junction of Bath Place, Lord Street and Parade Street. The Royalty Cinema, Peveril Hotel and Sea Terminal are in the centre and right background. (AC)

Right: In later years, Nos. 31-33 received the amended style of fleet name and larger fleet numbers and lost the black finish on the mudguards as seen in this Lord Street view of No.32. All three members of this batch remained in service until 1982 under the auspices of Isle of Man National Transport with No. 33 being withdrawn slightly earlier than the other two following the discovery of a crack in the chassis. (AC)

The next buses to join the fleet, in 1961, were three more Leyland Tiger Cubs, 3680-3682 MN, receiving fleet numbers 54-56.
These differed from the previous Tiger Cubs in that they had Willowbrook dual-purpose bodywork with coach-style seats for 41 passengers.
In a somewhat retrograde step, while the Weymann Cubs had electric door gear, on the Willowbrook Cubs this was operated by means of a large lever mounted on the cab floor.

Tiger Cub No. 56 inside Homefield Depot with an unidentified Olympic behind. Note the coach seats fitted to the Willowbrook-bodied Tiger Cubs.
(AC)

Leyland Tiger Cub No.56 in original livery with the Sea Terminal under construction in the background. (AC)

Tiger Cubs Nos.54-56 received grey and red coach livery in 1967 and also adopted much smaller fleet names as seen in this view of No. 55 in Lord Street Bus Station. (AC)

Tiger Cubs Nos.54-56 lost their coach livery and seats in 1973 and were repainted red and cream, receiving yet another change of fleet name. All three were withdrawn from service in 1979/80. (AC)

Opposite: Further Leyland Titan PD3s arrived in 1964. Though often referred to in various publications as PD3A/1s, denoting an air-braked version, they were in fact equipped with vacuum brakes, making them type PD3A/3, and internal company documents refer to them as such. Originally allocated fleet numbers 59-61 and registered 6-8 MAN, they were visibly different to preceding batches as the Metro-Cammell Weymann bodywork was fitted with red mudguards from new and fibreglass moulded 'St Helens' fronts (hence the 'A' suffix in the type designation) - so named after the first operator to take the new style incorporating a lowered bonnet section to improve the driver's view to the nearside.

These were the last new buses to carry A.M. Sheard's name as General Manager. As with previous versions of PD3s, these buses regularly recorded fuel consumption figures in the region of 11.4 miles per gallon – something that many modern vehicles would fail to achieve. (MNH) Leyland Titan PD3s Nos. 59-61 posed in Douglas Railway Station forecourt shortly after delivery.

Above: PD3 No.67 (originally No.60) parked in the afternoon sun with Olympic No. 50 opposite Homefield Garage in Salisbury Street, Douglas. (AC)

Below: By the time this photo was taken, No. 59 had become No. 69 and was re-registered 69 UMN. It had also lost its original fleet name in favour of the later style Road Services characters. (AC)

When the next deliveries occurred, there had been a change of management within Isle of Man Road Services. The company's first General Manager (originally Manager and Secretary), A.M. (Mylie) Sheard died in office in June 1965 and was succeeded by W.T. (Bill) Lambden.

Originally from Hampshire, Bill had been in the British Army, stationed at Port St. Mary, during World War Two and met and married a local girl, Gwelda Crowe from Kirk Michael.

He had come, not from another transport undertaking as might have been expected, but from being the editor of a transport publication, 'Bus and Coach'. His appointment proved to be a particularly happy choice for the company, however, as he was not only very familiar with the Island and its transport systems but was also very well liked and highly regarded.

The first vehicles purchased under Bill Lambden's management were seven former Aldershot & District Dennis Falcons with Strachan's 30 seat bodywork. New in 1956, the Falcons received fleet numbers 23-29 and were registered 23-29 HMN. (ML)

Dennis Falcon No. 23 clearly shows its Aldershot & District origin in this 1967 image taken at Cronk-y-Voddy. (ML)
Acquired as replacements for the wartime Bedford OWBs, they entered service in 1967 and were the last buses to receive the old-style fleet names and logos. These may well have been in short supply at the time as several of the batch received hand-painted fleet names as a temporary measure. Indeed, such was the urgency of getting the Falcons into service that five out of the seven did so still in their Aldershot green livery.

A 1975 view taken at the rear of Ramsey Bus Station showing three of the Dennis Falcons withdrawn from service and awaiting disposal.

Nearest the camera, No. 29 was rescued for preservation while the remainder were eventually scrapped.

Falcon No. 29 was subsequently exported to the UK where it was fully restored to original condition and reunited with its original registration POR 428 as Aldershot & District No. 282. (See inset) (AC)

Also delivered in 1967, were three new Leyland Leopards fitted with Willowbrook 41-seat dual-purpose bodywork.

The first vehicles to be delivered in the new grey and red coach livery, they received fleet numbers 96-98 and were registered 696-698 HMN.

Used initially for tours and airport limited stop services, they were well liked by the drivers as they were easy to handle at just over 30 feet in length and with Leyland's O600 9.8 litre engine they were capable of achieving 50 miles per hour.

In this photo, No.97 waits for a private party outside Peel Town Hall with one of the 1968 batch of Leopards (34-36) parked behind. (ML)

Left: Leopard No. 98 departs from Ronaldsway Airport with a Ribble Holiday Tour.

In the left background, a Leyland Royal Tiger is engaged on the regular airport service. Note the transitional new style font used in the fleet name. This was soon changed to a larger logo with different font. (MNH)

Below: Leopard No. 96 showing the effective way the boot panel was used to promote the company. The scene is Mines Road, Laxey with the famous 'Lady Isabella' water wheel in the right background. (MNH)

Left: Road Services' venture into coaching was not as successful as had been hoped and at the end of the 1971 season, Leopards 96-98 were withdrawn from service and transferred to Tours (IOM) operation where they were repainted green and cream and took fleet numbers 26-28. The photo shows 697 HMN in service with Tours in July 1972 parked alongside the Air Terminal building in Lord Street, Douglas. (AC)

Below: Another change took place in March 1973 when the three Willowbrook-bodied Leopards returned to Road Services and assumed their original fleet numbers.

While retaining their coach seats, they did not return to grey and red livery but instead adopted the standard fleet colours as shown with Leopard No. 96 at Lord Street Bus Station. All three Leopards remained in service until 1986. No. 97 was bought straight out of service by the author in February 1986 and remains in his ownership. (AC)

Below: Three more Leyland Leopards arrived in 1968, also in grey and red livery, though this time with Duple Commander 41-seat coach bodywork. They were issued with registration numbers 34-36 LMN and took fleet numbers 34-36.

These and subsequent coach deliveries were acquired in collaboration with UK operator Eastern National and, as with the previous batch, they did not stay long with Road Services and were transferred to Tours (Isle of Man) in 1972. The trio stayed with Tours until 1983 when they were sold for further use in Southern Ireland. Leopard No. 34, as delivered, waits to depart with a tour from outside the Villa Marina on Harris Promenade, Douglas. (AC)

Left: Leopard No. 34 with a party of happy holidaymakers in this 1970 view at St.Marks. (ML)

Below: In a departure from normal practice, the three Duple-bodied Leopards only carried Road Services logos on the boot panels as shown in this 1970 view near the Sound. (ML)

1970 saw the arrival of two more new coaches, followed by a further two in 1971. In both cases, these were a rare departure from Leyland manufacture, being Bristol RELH6Ls – the first two with Duple 49-seat coach bodywork and the second two with bodywork by Plaxton.

All four were delivered in grey and red. By this time, the Island was feeling the effects of a diminishing tourist trade and the coaching arm of the business proved to be less lucrative than had been hoped. Once again, they enjoyed a very short time in Road Services employment.

The two Duple-bodied examples were withdrawn in 1973 and sold to a UK operator while the Plaxtons were transferred to Tours (Isle of Man) in 1971.

Though manufactured by Bristol, the REs came with Leyland O.680 engines and were plagued with overheating problems especially when tackling the climb up the Mountain Road from Ramsey. The cause was eventually traced to the small diameter of the water pipes connecting the rear-mounted engine with the front-mounted radiator. But by then it was too late.

This May 1970 image shows the first two Bristol REs arriving at Douglas aboard the Isle of Man Steam Packet Company's freight vessel *Peveril*. At that time, the ship was equipped with two 10-ton electric cranes (later removed) and one of these is seen in action unloading No. 37 while No. 38 awaits its turn across the deck. The effect of the uneven weight distribution due to the rear-mounted engine is obvious in this photo. (MNH)

A 1970 view of Bristol RE No. 37 taken on the Mountain Road looking down onto the northern plain with the Point of Ayre in the far distance. Compare the marked difference in body style of the Duple bodywork (again with Road Services lettering absent from the side panels) with the following photos of the Plaxton-bodied REs. (ML)

Bristol REs No. 39 and No. 40 also arrived aboard Peveril the following year, 1971. In this case, the new-style larger fleet names were already applied to the side panels on delivery. (SB)

Bristol RE No. 40 with a Greenslades Holiday Tour at the bottom of Broadway. Author's note: Readers might notice the striking similarity of the photographer to a well-known TV personality of the time,(Alan Whicker). (AC)

Another vehicle acquired in 1971, was a Bedford SB coach, NMN 218. Twenty years old by the time it came to Road Services from Crennell's Garage, Ramsey, it was not used and passed straight to Tours who sold it the following year to an Irish operator.

More second-hand vehicles followed in 1971 and 1972 with a total of fifteen Leyland Titan PD3s, which had been new to Stratford Blue and latterly in service with Birmingham & Midland Motor Omnibus Company (BMMO). The new arrivals can be summarized as follows:

Nos. 41-43 PD3/4 Willowbrook bodywork (exposed radiator), new 1960, registered MN 41-43, acquired November 1971.

Nos. 57-60 PD3/4 NCME (Northern Counties Motor & Engineering) bodywork (exposed radiator), new 1963, registered MN 57-60, acquired December, 1971

Nos. 44-45 PD3A/1 Willowbrook bodywork (St Helens front), new 1963, registered MN 44-45, acquired January 1972.

Nos. 63-66 PD3A/1 Willowbrook, (St Helens front) new 1963, registered MN 63-66, acquired September, 1972.

Nos. 70-71 PD3A/1 Willowbrook, (St Helens front) new 1966, registered MN 2670-2671, acquired September, 1972.

These relatively youthful front-entrance vehicles arrived already painted in Road Services livery and with fleet names and numbers applied. They proved to be a very good buy and gave years of largely trouble-free service to the company.

Top: Leyland Titan PD3/4 No. 41, the first of the ex-Stratford Blue/BMMO PD3s, parked at Lord Street Bus Station, Douglas. (AC)
Above: PD3/4 No. 42, also at Lord Street Bus Station with Tiger Cub No. 55 and PD3 XMN 347 behind. Compare the original opening cab window on No. 41 with the replacement fixed glass on No. 42. (AC)

Leyland PD3/4 No. 57 approaching Bath Place roundabout shows its illuminated upper-deck advertising panel with which it was equipped on arrival. (AC)

One of the second-hand acquisitions arriving on the Island in 1972, PD3A/1 No. 45, shows the considerable difference in front-end appearance with its 'St Helens' front while loading passengers at Castletown. (AC)

Northern Counties-bodied PD3/4, No. 57 sits in the afternoon sun at Lord Street Bus Station. After passing to Isle of Man National Transport, three of this batch, Nos. 57-59, were subsequently converted to open top but saw very little use on passenger duties with No. 59 spending some time as a tree-lopper. (AC)

The last of the NCME PD3/4s, No. 60, retained its roof until withdrawal from service in 1981. The sliding cab door – a feature much appreciated by drivers on a hot summer day - is readily apparent in this view taken at Lord Street Bus Station. One of the ex-Douglas Corporation Transport Willowbrook-bodied Bedford YRQs can be seen in the left background. (AC)

Above: Leyland PD3A/1 No. 65 with a variety of Road Services and Douglas Corporation Transport buses at Lord Street Bus Station. (AC)

Below: One of this type, No. 64, was converted into a tow bus in National Transport days but its career was cut short when its rear end was mangled in a collision with ex-Ribble Leopard No. 7 which was under tow following a breakdown.

The PD3 was scrapped but the Leopard was repaired and returned to service. Remarkably, Leopard No. 7 still survives in preservation. (AC)

With a St Helens front and larger destination aperture, PD3A/1 No. 66 with Willowbrook bodywork is pictured at Lord Street Bus Station. (AC)

The last of the fifteen ex-BMMO PD3A/1s, No. 71, pauses between duties at Lord Street. Most of these lasted in service until the late 1970s, or early 80s, by which time they were in the region of twenty years old. (AC)

Something completely different to arrive in 1974 was a Leyland National 11351/1R, originally registered MN 9514 and given fleet number 14, it was re-registered MAN 14A in May 1974.

The Leyland National featured bodywork formed of pressed-steel panels riveted together to make a fairly rigid shell.

It was a bold concept embodying a number of features not previously seen on Road Services buses such as a rear-mounted turbo-charged engine with a fixed cylinder head, air suspension, power steering and a semi-automatic gearbox. At 11.3 metres, the National was also significantly longer than anything else in the fleet.

Leyland National No. 14 on a pre-delivery test-run in the UK. Note the all-red livery (apart from the bumpers) adopted by this new class of vehicle. The Nationals appeared to be a slightly darker shade of red than hitherto, though this may have been due to differences in paint batches or fading of the paintwork on the older vehicles – something to which red is particularly prone. (ML)

National No. 14 was only two years old when it was absorbed into the newly created Isle of Man National Transport Ltd fleet, with only a change of fleet name and legal lettering required to complete the transformation. (AC)

Later in 1974, a further ten second-hand Leyland PD3s were taken into the fleet. These again were of the PD3A/1 type and had been new to Bournemouth Corporation Transport in 1963. Unlike previous batches, this delivery had Weymann bodywork and although painted in Road Services' colours they came without fleet names or numbers and still sported their original registration numbers.

Some members of the batch are seen arriving at Douglas aboard *Peveril*. (ML)

The ex-Bournemouth PD3s received fleet numbers 72-81 and were registered LMN 72–81. These, again, proved to be a good buy and continued in service with Road Services' successors, Isle of Man National Transport and Isle of Man Passenger Transport until 1983. (ML)

The Willowbrook bodywork on former Bournemouth Corporation PD3A/1s No. 72 and No. 73 is shown to good effect in this photo taken at Lord Street Bus Station. Though never fully utilised by Road Services, the comprehensive destination displays available can be seen in this view. (AC)

Top: Six more new Leyland Nationals, arrived in 1975 receiving fleet numbers 15–20 and registrations MAN 15D–20D.

Below: One of the 1975 batch, MAN 16D is craned off the Isle of Man Steam Packet ship Peveril at Douglas. (ML)

On this page and overleaf are two views of National No. 22 at Lord Street Bus Station in 1976. In the first view, the Steam Packet's electric crane can be seen working in the background while on the far left is one of the electronic guides showing a map of Douglas with push-button illumination of points of interest. (TLP)

In the second view, National No. 22 poses with Tiger Cub No. 54, while the chimney of Noble's Baths, situated on Victoria Street, can be seen in the left background. (TLP)

The final deliveries received by Isle of Man Road Services were seven Leyland Nationals in 1976, carrying fleet numbers 21–27 and registered MAN 21H–27H.

One of the last Road Services' acquisitions was National No. 26, seen in this 1976 view shortly before nationalisation, with Peel Castle in the background.
Although not universally popular with staff, the Nationals proved themselves more durable than had been expected and most had a service life in the region of twenty years. (MNH)

Six more Nationals, Nos. 28-33, MAN 28N–33N, ordered by Road Services, arrived the following year by which time Road Services and Douglas Corporation Transport had been amalgamated under government control to form Isle of Man National Transport but that is another story…

Bill Lambden stands on the rear platform of a former Douglas Corporation AEC Regent V soon after the formation of Isle of Man National Transport in 1976. (ML)

Though Bill Lambden, who had been the last Road Services General Manager, went on to become the first Isle of Man National Transport General Manager upon its formation on 1st October 1976, his term was cut short by his sudden and untimely death in 1978. What might have become of the nationalised bus undertaking had he lived will never be known but given the circumstances of diminishing tourism and lack of investment at the time, it seems unlikely that even he could have brought about a return to profitability. Bill was followed into the bus and coach industry by his oldest son Mike who spent 47 years working for National Bus Company and National Express and who has very kindly provided many of the pictures used in this book.